documenti d'Arte

Rome, the Forums

Stefano Maggi

ISTITUTO GEOGRAFICO DE AGOSTINI

Original title
Roma, i Fori

English Translation by
Robert Mercurio

This series is under the direction of
Silvio Locatelli and Marcella Boroli

Editing
Silvia Broggi, Ersilia Lombardini

Captions
by the editorial staff

Secretary to the editorial staff
Wanda Bonaccini

Graphics and layout
Otello Geddo, Giancarlo Elli

Arrangement of illustrations
Centro Iconografico of the
Istituto Geografico De Agostini - Milan

The photographs in this book are by A. DE GREGO-
RIO with the exception of those on the following pages which are by SCALA: 24-25, 27, 29, 37 (a, b), 38-
39, 42-43 (a, b), 44, 45, 54-55, 63, 73.

Catalogo 24614

Pubblicazione a volumi quindicinali
Registrazione Tribunale di Novara n. 24 del 28/11/1980

Direttore responsabile
Emilio Bucciotti

An Admirable Monument to Peace and Harmony

In virtue of the number of functions which it fulfilled, the Roman forum represents one of the fullest expressions of human coexistence in the ancient world. It is comparable to the Greek *agorá*. Both of these were in fact open spaces to be used for public life; but the concept of the forum went even further in that there was no separation of the civil sphere from the religious one, and the latter of these two was called upon to emphasize the various manifestations of public life. This phenomenon was not always to be found in Greece.

The forum is to be seen then as a typically Roman creation, both in view of what has already been said, and taken as an urbanistic and architectonic reality, even though it was undoubtedly influenced by the technical, practical and artistic heritage of Greece and by the engineering experience of the Etruscans.

The forum is one of the principal components of every Roman city and even though it is impossible to generalize, it can be said to be one of its least variable elements in terms of form.

The Roman forum came to be something unique, the «forum» par excellence not so much because of its architectonic showiness, or at least not only because of this, but because of the evolution, modification and enrichment which its historical-cultural significance underwent, having been first a symbol of republican liberty and democracy, then of the Empire and of the dynasty of the princes. This great urbanistic structure, realized in the course of various generations, cannot be enclosed within any one definition but should rather be seen as the sum of single components and contributions placed one upon the other in the course of time. And also the successive Imperial fora should be seen from this same point of view: creations, like the Roman forum, which were evocative, full of monuments which "spoke" to the citizens of Rome and of the Empire and which still 'speak", even though in a somewhat mutilated manner, to the modern man who wishes to turn an ear to that ancient world which generated our culture.

As far as spatial organization and the arrangement of architectonic forms is concerned the Roman forum was conditioned by the situations and by the historical, political and cultural happenings which characterized the phenomenon of the growth of Rome's power, first along the "provincial" horizon of Italy, and then throughout the Hellenistic Mediterranean basin. It was born as a function of the meeting of two roads — the one crossing the Tiber and the one following up along this river — in order to satisfy two of man's most urgent needs, those of encounter and exchange, both materially and spiritually speaking.

Its topographical location, between the inhabited area of the Palatine and that of the Campidoglio-Quirinal (the most ancient ones in Rome) allowed it to quickly assume a communitarian aspect, both politically and religiously. And since, as is now commonly recognized, the Etruscan intervention of the VII century gave the ethnic groups that lived in separate villages that unity which led to the development of an urban civilization, we shouldn't be surprised to find that the structural genesis of the forum is also to be found in the period of the Etruscan monarchy.

The sources do in fact tell us of reclamation projects carried out in the valleys, under Tarquinius Priscus, the first Etruscan king of Rome. Among these projects was the channelling of the waters of the plain of the forum by means of the *Cloaca Maxima*.

At the spot where this entered what was to become the Roman forum, we find the ruins of a sacellum to Venus and Cloacina, the latter probably being an ancient water divinity. Thanks to this reclamation, this area, which until the VII century had been used for necropoli, was able to be used as public space for the various institutions of community living; the first paving of this area (end of the VII century) is almost contemporaneous with the sudden end of funereal interments here.

We know very little about this period and about the period of the monarchy in general. It was characteristic of ancient civilizations to look to their origins, to those uncertain periods cloacked in legend as to a sort of "Golden Age". Rome was no exception, and its historians who were engaged in the study of these origins — even those who lived in a political and social environment which seemed to refuse the monarchical regime and even detested it — could not help referring to personages from those times, suspended somewhere between myth and history, these being institutions and customs which were, by tradition, dear to the Romans. And so, as regards the foundation of the most ancient buildings of the forum, of which, in most cases, nothing remains but a venerable name, we also find the equally venerable names of Titus Tazius, Numa Pompilius, Servius Tullius, ...

The functions of the forum

We can affirm with certainty that already in those times the two main functions of the forum, the economic-social one and the political-religious one, were concentrated in two distinct areas; the market-place was to the south and the *Comitium* to the north at the foot of the Campidoglio.

An indication of the commercial activities can be seen in the various *tabernae*, real shops which rose up alongside the most important buildings of the republican era and of which a large number were still active at least until the end of the first era of the Empire.

The *Comitium*, as the term itself suggests, represented the meeting place of the citizens' assembly: during the period of the monarchy, this was used for the meetings of the curie, into the thirty sections of which the three noble tribes of the Tamnensi, the Tiziense and the Lucerni were divided for military and political reasons. But two factors would seem to suggest that the *Comitium* was at one and the same time a sacred place: first of all, the location of the Sanctuary of Jove on the Campidoglio which conferred upon the area below it the value of *templum*, that is of a space dedicated to a divinity; secondly, the archaeological remains of the *Lapis Niger* (black stone), the sanctuary-tomb of Romulus.

But the sacred character of the entire area is evidenced above all by the Temple of Vesta which, as the excavations have indicated, was built almost at the same time as the foundation of the city (the traditional date is 754-753 B.C.). In this temple, the sacred fire, symbol of the life of Rome, was kept. This could never be allowed to go out, and at first its care was entrusted, according to tradition, to the daughters of the king, and then to the vestal virgins, six in number, the real priestesses of the city, about whose virtue and courage many legends have come down to us.

In the most secret part of the temple, the relics brought by the mythical Aeneas from distant Troy were kept, and among these the famous Palladio, simulacrum of Minerva, stood out.

Next to the Temple of Vesta stood another important edifice, the *Regia*, the royal residence founded by Numa Pompilius, according to tradition. The most ancient phases of the construction of this building seem to go back to the VII and VI centuries, and not even the coming of the republican era marked an end to the use and enjoyment of the edifice. It simply underwent a restructuralization of form, which is the one that has come down to us, and in this place the *rex sacrorum* and the *pontifex maximus* carried out the religious functions they inherited from the king. For us, the most important of these was the editing of the annals. In addition, the shields sacred to Mars were kept in the *Regia*.

Tradition has assigned the foundation of the Sanctuary of Janus to Numa Pompilius as well; this was the "indicator of peace and of war" for when the doors of this rectangular construction similar to an arch (some hold it to be an ancient gate of the city) were open, peace reigned in the world. This however happened rarely according to ancient sources; only twice before Augustus, the restorer of the Pax Romana. This sanctuary was probably located at the southern entrance of the Argiletum, but no traces remain of it. We have only a pale reflection of it on a coin of Nero's.

It seems possible on the other hand to pick out some traces of the *Volcanal*, the altar of Vulcan, which was located among the ancient sanctuaries of Rome. These traces can be found in some cracks in the tufa near the *Comitium*, in the vicinity of the Arch of Septimius Severus. This altar is traditionally attributed to Titus Tazius, the king of the Sabines who inhabited the Quirinal hill and whose women were abducted by the mythical founder of Rome. Later, on the occasion of the ratification of the pact between Titus Tazius and Romulus which sanctioned the peace and unification of the Sabines with the Latins, not only was this altar erected, but the name Via Sacra was also given to that road which crossed the area of the forum at the bottom of the valley between the Campidoglio and the Velia hills, along a west-east axis at the foot of the Palatine and which was solemnly processed on that occasion by the two kings.

The change of regime, from the monarchy to the republic (the traditional date is 509 B.C.) did not bring with it any abrupt change in the urbanistic development of the forum, but simply a progressive increase and strengthening of the structures, in close relation with the new institutions and the general growth of Rome.

The *Comitium* apparently took on a regular shape, circular in this case, onto which looked various edifices emblematic of the Roman constitution: the *Curia Hostilia*, the meeting place of the Senate (tradition attributes this to Tullus Hostilius, as the name indicates), which was destroyed by fire in 52 B.C. and replaced by the *Curia Iulia* begun by Caesar and completed by Augustus in 29 B.C.; the *Senaculum*, another meeting place of the senators; the *Graecostasis*, a tribune reserved for foreign ambassadors, most of whom were Greek speaking which explains the name; the *Rostra*, the tribune from which the magistrates spoke and which from 338 B.C. was decorated with the rostra of the ships which were captured from the Latin coalition at Anzio.

In the years immediately following the change of regime, some of the most important sanctuaries of the city rose up in the forum, thereby emphasizing the close relationship between the religious and political spheres. Among these were the Temple of

Saturn (501-493 B.C.) and the Temple of the Dioscuri or of the Castors (484 B.C.).

The first of these temples commemorated the mythical city founded by this god on the hill at the foot of which the temple was located. The Saturnali were celebrated on the 17 December in this honour. This was an end-of-the-year celebration, similar in some aspects to our celebration of Carneval. Within this temple the public treasury was probably kept. The second of these two temples was built in fulfillment of a promise made after the battle of Lake Regillo (497-496 B.C.) in which the Roman troops, led by Aulus Postumius Albinus, defeated the Latins and the Volsci thus allowing the city to emerge brilliantly from the period of crisis which the Etruscan decadence had created within the delicate balance of relations existing among the peoples of central Italy, and to establish the foundations for that hegemony which Rome was soon to impose upon the entire peninsula. Legend credits two obscure horsemen, identified with the Dioscuri, Castor and Pollux, with a large part of the responsibility for this victory. This was an important cult in the Magna Grecia, and its presence here attests to the effective development of trade which had been reached, especially by sea. In time, this temple became the focal point of an important civil ceremony, for in front of it passed the parade in which each year the equestrian order presented the new knights to the censors. Then the union of the sacred and the profane, characteristic of the forum in general, was emphasized by the fact that the temple was also the seat of the office of weights and measures. The cult of the Dioscuri was related to that of Giuturna, goddess protectress of the waters, because at the font of the same name, just east of the spot where the temple stood, the two horsemen came to water their horses and announce the victory to the Romans. The Font of Giuturna, together with the *Lacus Curtius*, are evidence of the original swampy state of the valley of the forum.

At the end of the V century and for all of the IV century Rome was engaged in arduous struggles with its neighbours, such as the war with Veio (477-396 B.C.), the Gallic invasion (390 B.C.), the southern Etruscan coalition (389-350 B.C.), and the Samnite Wars (343-341, 325-304 B.C.). This difficult political and military situation explains the absence of any building activity in the forum in this period. The only example of any such activity is the Temple of Concordia (367 B.C.), built by the dictator Camillus who liberated Rome from the Gauls. This temple commemorated the end of the struggle between the patricians and the plebeians, a struggle which had reached its most bitter moment in the secession of the plebeians to the Aventine hill — apologue of Menenius Agrippa — in 494 B.C., the creation of the courts for the plebeians, and the promulgation of the laws of the XII tables (451-450 B.C.). These episodes came to a happy conclusion with the laws of C. Licinius Stolone and L. Sestius (367 B.C.) which guaranteed the right of the plebeians to hold the office of consul.

The gods and the history of Rome

From all that has been said so far, one thing has clearly emerged: the cults which were celebrated in the forum were closely connected with the history of the city, and their edifices were reminders of important episodes from it, such as its foundation (*Lapis Niger*, Temple of Saturn), and dramatic moments for its very survival to which heroic or supernatural events were linked (Temple of Vesta, Temple of Castors), etc.

By honouring the gods, one did in fact honour the greatness of Rome and of its citizens. It was, we might say, a kind of civic religiosity permeating this entire area which was intended for the political and economic activity of this democratic common life. What emerges then is one of the loftiest characteristics of the Roman mentality: its calling to the *monumentum* (i.e. that which immortalizes a memory). The forum becomes, in its entirety, *monumentum* of the city, it immortalizes its history.

From this same standpoint, one must interpret the fact that for the buildings in the forum we know the names of the persons who had them built, but not of the architects who actually built them. And from this same perspective we should view the numerous monuments erected in the central area of the forum to illustrious personages.

It was not until the end of the war against the Latins and the Capuans (338 B.C.) that Rome ceased to be a "provincial" phenomenon. The consequence of this war was the setting up of direct contact with the cities of Campania which had a Greek culture. In the III century, in the period between the second and third Punic Wars, Rome presented itself on the Mediterranean front and having become an imperialistic power, felt the need to celebrate its own prestige and to restructure its order of buildings. It is here then that we find the foundations for the monumentalization of the forum, made feasible through contact with the Hellenistic conceptions of architecture. The greatest development in this new tendency was to come in the II century, after the Punic Wars and the wars of the Orient.

The localization of the functions of the forum was perfected. The economic ones passed largely to other areas — only the shops of the bankers and other luxury items remained — and the political and administrative functions required more space. These activities spread out from the *Comitium* towards the south and the east with new buildings in which there was a sort of mutual adaptation of Greek forms and Roman content. In the field of religious architecture, by nature conservative, we have the restoration of the Temple of Concordia (121 B.C., L. Opimi) and of the Temple of the Castors (117 B.C., L. Cecilius Metellus Dalmaticus); in this field however faithfulness was maintained to the traditional type of italic temple, elevated on a high podium with heavy accentuation of the main front and the resulting preferential point of view. (We have only very scarce traces of these restoration projects since others were then carried out in the Augustan era).

There was more scope for innovation in the field of civil architecture, this being the sphere which logically had to follow more closely the social and political evolution in progress. A good example of this is the powerful appearance of the basilica, a civil construction whose purpose was to house all of the economic and administrative "operations" in those seasons marked by inclement weather. Four of these were built in the arc of a sixty year period: the Basilica Porcia in 184, the Basilica Aemilia in 179, the Basilica Sempronia in 170 and finally the Basilica Olimpia in 121 B.C.

The form of the basilica was probably derived from the Greeks in southern Italy, but it was reinterpreted here in a very functional way. The result, both simple and original, was a rectangular edifice, not open on one of its short sides but along one of its long sides in a colonnade which made the internal space a continuation of the forum itself, almost a covered forum.

It is likely that there is an indirect link between the basilica and the Royal Portico of the *agorá* of Athens as far as architectonic typology is concerned, and it would also seem that as far as the total visual effect of the setting is concerned, there is an analogy with the Hellenistic arrangement of squares in general. The planning and layout of the forum received with the basilica, in addition to its practical aspect, a thrust in the direction of the regular ordering and monumentalization of the entire complex. This setting harmonized well with the façades of the temples looking onto the square and also with another imposing edifice, the *Tabularium* built to be the seat of the State Archives by Q. Lutazius Catulus on the slopes of the Capitoline hill at the beginning of the I century B.C.

Radical transformations

The Punic Wars and the wars of the Orient resulted in a disproportion of wealth between, on the one hand, the old senatorial, militaristic aristocracy and the new entrepreneuring bourgeoise class, and on the other hand, the mass of the farmers and proletariat. The investment of capital in land holdings and the parallel weakening of the farmer class, who represented the real strength of the army, brought about a crisis which was not only agricultural and economic, but also political and institutional.

One of the results was that the army, formerly composed of farmers, became professional. Since the army represented the greatest organized force in existence in Rome, its leaders not only represented the military power of the State, but were to become its political leaders as well, thus depriving both the Senate and the popular assembly of their political authority. And with the crisis of the Republic and the passing of power into the hands of potentially monarchical elements, we can witness by means of urbanistic restructuralization, a change in the functions of the forum.

The reconstruction of the Basilica Sempronia, the construction of the great new Basilica Julia and the restoration of the Basilica Aemilia (probably in 54 B.C.), all by Caesar, can be seen in terms of the previously mentioned tendency to organize space more regularly. But a radical transformation was carried out by the dictator in the area of the *Comitium*, and this had obvious political significance. The *Curia Hostilia* of the republican tradition disappeared, and the new *Curia Iulia* occupied a part of the area of the *Comitium* itself. This was later to become an annex of the Forum of Caesar which was under construction. The senate thus lost its power, and this power passed into the hands of one man. The *Rostra* were moved into positions which were axial in relation to the rectangular space between the two basilicas, on the western side of the square. Even if the reason for this was the practical need of setting up a larger meeting area, it was also at the same time an unmistakable sign of the definitive decline of the republican *Comitium*.

But the decisive event was the realization of a new forum, the Julian forum, begun by the dictator and completed by his adopted son, Octavian Augustus. This constituted the official celebration of the power and charism of the Caesars and became the seed from which the entire complex of the Imperial fora grew.

In this complex the idea of a clearly defined rectangular space, which had been experimented with in the arrangement of the fora in some of the colonies, was applied, but it had to be adapted to the available area. The main axis was elongated providing a view in perspective of the 6-columned temple to Venus Genetrix, ancient progenetrix of the dictator's family, which was raised on a podium. The presence of shops along the south side is evidence that the idea of the forum as fulfilling a number of social functions was still present. But it is also clear that the aim of increasing the space for public use was subordinated, in peremptory fashion, to the desire to celebrate, propagandize and impose the idea of charismatic power. The temple was of course the ideal completion of the entire complex, but a second pole, and a more evident one, was represented by the equestrian statue of Caesar which could not but attract the public's attention, located there in the centre of the square.

Architectonically speaking, the Temple of Venus Genetrix is interesting for a number of reasons. The traditional approach to the idea of putting a sacred edifice on a platform to be viewed frontally underwent two innovative variations: first of all, the completion of the cella in an absidal form, a motif which was to enjoy special favour in the imperial era and later; and secondly, the covering of the cella itself, most probably with a cement vault. In an age which was witnessing the triumph of the classicism of marble, this was one of the few real structural applications — and not simply substructural (podium) — of construction techniques which was to represent for a century or perhaps more, one of the great conquests of Roman engineering, and which is even the basis for modern building.

A large part of the forum underwent two massive restorations. The more important, carried out under Trajan, should be seen in relation to the work for a new forum, and it was also to lead to the addition, in the south-western corner, of the Basilica Argentaria, which was probably the seat of a school. The other restoration project was carried out under Diocletian.

Art as celebration

The advent of Augustus seemed to mark a real political revolution: the new State wanted to distinguish itself as, or at least appear as, the restoration of the ancient one, but it was in fact a new product, the result of civil wars, and its principal elements turned out to be the army and its commander.

The revolution brought with it a form of absolute power which had to be both justified and propagandized throughout the Empire, and Augustus understood how art played a didactic, illustrative and celebrative role and therefore how it could serve as the vehicle for his propagandistic message.

His urbanistic projects had, as their starting point, Caesar's projects, and he first of all completed the forum of his adopted father. He then supervised the construction of the Temple to Divus Julius (divinization after death was a custom among Hellenistic and eastern monarchies), on the eastern side of the Roman forum, and the construction of the Basilica Julia in which the technique of opus caementicium was applied on the vaults of the internal galleries instead of the wooden covering, which was limited to the central hall.

But his project found its fullest development in the construction of a new forum. Caesar's Forum served as the inspiration and model for the Forum of Augustus, constructed to satisfy that same need for space (seeing as administrative activity was continually increasing) but also with that same intention of celebrating himself. We find here once again the rectangular layout, elongated and closed at the sides by a columned portico which leads the eye up along a well-designed and measured out perspective line to the temple dedicated to *Mars Ultor*, that is to Mars as avenger of the Caesar's death. At the centre of the square the quadriga of Augustus stood out. In its organization and decoration, this forum turned out to be, rather than an open affirmation of personal power, an admirable monument to peace and harmony, the message of a man who kept his monarchical ideas veiled behind the appearances of respect for tradition. And tradition, in Rome, meant Republic.

The porticos on the sides of the temple curved inwards in two exedrae and suggested with their circular form the idea of harmony. These exedrae were "populated" by statues of personages such as Aeneas, Julus and all the offspring of the Giulii to the south, of Romulus and the outstanding men of the Republic on the north side, and this produced a subtle mixture of the *gens Iulia* with the history of Rome. And so in practice, by celebrating the grandeur of Rome, one was also celebrating the greatness of those who, as heirs of Julius, had brought the power of Rome to its apogee.

The centripetal tendency of the forum, as a space closed in upon itself, was accentuated; it was closed off from the outside by a high wall with two arched entrances (the value of this type of construction as a demarcation is well-known).

In the realization of these projects, the real value of that famous phrase of Augustus' is evident: "I received a Rome of bricks, I gave back to you a Rome of marble". The widespread use of the white marble of Carrara did in fact enter public construction, and since it was a valuable material, it was used as an outer covering for the tufa rock.

In the fora of Caesar and of Augustus, the dimensions of the buildings tended to be smaller (this is largely explainable in terms of the high cost of land) and to assume classical dimensions which did not suffocate the traditional constructions nor disturb the physical and environmental surroundings. The restructuralization of the Roman forum was, in terms of its results, in line with this urbanistic plan. In the Roman forum too, with the construction of the Arch of Augustus and that of Gaius and Lucius, which were real dividers between the square and the rest of the area, the concept of the forum as an internal space which did not look out onto anything was accentuated, along with the desire to accomplish dynastic propaganda.

The counterpoint to the Arch of Augustus was to be the one constructed by Tiberius at the point where the Via Sacra leaves the forum and goes west.

The so-called Temple of Peace was a monumental complex of great interest. Built by Vespasian on the site of the ancient *Macellum* to celebrate and commemorate the re-establishment of peace following the harsh civil wars of 69 B.C. over the rulership, it was actually a real forum in itself. The general outline of the complex, which unfortunately has been almost completely destroyed, can be reconstructed from the fragments of the marble map of the city realized by Septimius Severus and placed in an end room which was reached from the portico on the right of the temple.

The spacious rectangular square was arranged as if a garden and surrounded by porticos. As a backdrop, but in a rather reserved manner, was the temple which, having no podium, was set in at the centre of the portico almost without interrupting the continuity of its line; the temple was noticeable only because its front was higher. It was flanked by libraries and galleries in which the trophies brought back from the war in Judea (71 A.D.) were displayed. These are depicted on the panels of the Arch of Titus. Also in the galleries were numerous works of art by Myron, Phidias, Naukydes, Leochares, Polycletus, Protogenes and Nicomachus.

Between the Forum of Augustus and that of Vespasian came, still in the Flavian epoch, the Forum Transitorium. This was almost entirely built under Domitian but inaugurated by Nerva. Its name indicates what its main characteristic was: that of being a topographical link between the fora, the Temple of Peace and the *Subura*. The long and narrow area which was available made it impossible to build a portico and in its place a series of large columns was set up almost right up against the boundary wall. These were connected by small architraves. The total visual effect was thereby saved and resolved and the Temple in the background, dedicated to Minerva, was highlighted, being as it was at the end of this axial perspective. This temple was constructed with the by now tried and tested technique of the apsed cella, and this curved motif was taken up again in the opposite direction by the horse-shoe shaped exedra which faced the *Subura*.

The building activity of the Flavian emperors also involved the Roman forum. In keeping with the aim of exalting the dynasty which had been imposed by Augustus with the insertion of the Temple of the Divus Julius, we find at the end of the century at the foot of the Campidoglio the almost symmetrical insertion of the Temple of the divi Vespasian and Titus. This is a prostyle 6-columned corinthian temple with a pediment decorated with the motif of sacrificial instruments. The cella here was widened in order to exploit the lack of space, a solution that had already been adopted in the nearby Temple of Concordia.

The large temple dedicated to Faustina (141 A.D.), the wife of Antoninus Pius, and after the death of this emperor also dedicated to his divinized name, was built with the same intent in mind. The majestic remains of this edifice — the columns in cipolin marble, capitals and architrave in the same white marble as the facade and pronaos, have been incorporated into the church of San Lorenzo in Miranda.

The old republican forum then lost all of its functions and became simply a place which represented dynastic ideals. It was to later contain even a colossal statue of Domitian (set up in 91 A.D.) while he was still living, an obvious sign of an attempt to affirm in a very direct manner the principle of imperial power. The statue was destroyed after the death of Domitian (96 A.D.) but two centuries later other monuments to the absolute power which was by now openly and clearly celebrated, were to appear: in 303 A.D. the honorary column which commemorated the tenth anniversary of the tetrarchy, the new form of government instituted by Diocletian which combined in the rulership two Augusti (Diocletian himself and Maximianus) and two Caesars (Galerius and Costanzo Clorus) as their designated successors; a few years later, the colossal statue of Constantine on the exact spot where the one of Domitian had stood; and finally, the Column of Foca, about which we shall have more to say later.

The forum as the exaltation of the emperor

The last and largest of the Imperial Fora was the Ulpian forum. This forum-market complex reveals a great unity of planning and construction which transcends the different architectural languages used for these two elements. As far as its position in the midst of the existing scenery is concerned, the former of these two elements necessitated the cutting away and levelling of the Quirinal hill thus causing a daring modification in the morphology of the land, while the latter created a sort of mask for these unnatural cuts, covering the division of the hill with a series of different levels, the total visual effect of which was exquisite. The unity of the complex can also be seen in the appearance and distribution of the different areas which seem to be carefully joined to one another along the well modulated line of demarcation which was marked out by the north-east portico with its hemicycle and by the apse of the Basilica Ulpia. From the utilitarian point of view, there was the coordination of the areas to be used for political and administrative purposes with those destined to be used as market-places and with educational spaces (auditorium), thus restoring the comprehensive value of the civic institutions which the forum had originally had. All of this was thanks to the great military architect of the emperor, Apollodorus of Damascus who had served under the emperor in the Dacic Wars.

In the intervention of Trajan in this area then we can find a number of meanings and ideas. First of all there was the ideological significance of this forum complex with its obvious political message: Trajan, the first great emperor from the provinces, a real war lord, harkens back in part to his great predecessor, Augustus, who founded this type of imperial power, but in part he also takes a certain distance from him. By adopting to a large extent the Augustan outline which celebrated the peace that had been given to men by the deity of the earth, he meant to point to that new peace which however this time had been imposed through the use of arms on the enemy.

There was a clear break with tradition here in that the temple disappeared and was replaced by the basilica. But this was probably a natural consequence of the evolution of the times, for whereas in the fora of Caesar and Augustus the temple constituted the architectonic focal point, the ideal one was without a doubt the statue of the emperor. Here, with the basilica replacing the temple, the architectonic perspective was renewed while the significance of the entire monumental complex was more simply expressed: the forum was to first and foremost exalt Trajan, lord of war and enlightened ruler. For the practical military mind then, the colossal statue of the emperor and the columns depicting his undertakings were sufficient. Apollodorus too referred back to military architecture, specifically to the *praetorium*, the most important part of a Roman encampment, in his design for the lay-out of the forum.

This great personality must have been involved as well in the conception of, if not in the decorative realization of, the famous coclidean column, in view of the close and subtle relation it reveals with the urbanistic project. The inscription on its base emphasizes in fact that the height of the column corresponds to that of the cut which had been made in the Quirinal hill. The problem of the architectonic framing and positioning of this monument was resolved completely in terms of height. One should note its precise location on a spot which, after the wall of the basilica, opens out once again, but in greatly reduced dimensions, between the two libraries and the temple. (This temple was consecrated by Hadrian to the divus Trajan, and we are not sure if it belonged to the original plan). In view of these reduced dimensions then the real opening is the upward one, along the fluid visual line marked out by the spiral of the column and culminating in the most logical of conclusions, the statue of Trajan, as the tradition of honorary columns would have it.

This is the first important, official work in which we find a liberation from the weight of the Greek tradition. Even if the idea of a column as a support for a statue had been tried and tested before, the idea of covering its shaft with a continuous spiral band some 200 metres long was completely new. The relief tells the story of episodes from the two Dacic Wars (101-102 and 105-107 A.D.). These wars, as a part of the expansionistic movements towards the orient, led to the formation of a new province, rich in gold and iron.

The figurative starting point for this entire monument has been located in the triumphal pictures which are of an extremely realistic nature. They are a detailed presentation of landscapes and customs in a language which though still in the tradition of Hellenistic realism, contained a more marked expressionism and a lessening of the organic cohesion of the whole. A pleasing balance was reached here between Greek artistic culture and the Latin-Italic expressive traditions, all in a style that was fully Roman.

Some reference was made earlier to the bipolarism of architectonic modes of expression. In the forum, the architectonic elements, as seen both in the planning and in the materials used, show a return to Augustan classicism. Conservatism thus mixed delicately and efficiently with the innovations in the layout.

The techniques used in the market-places were however new and of great importance for their development: the admirable organization of the complex in an upward direction and the appreciation and use of cement and of visible brick work. In keeping with the essentially utilitarian nature of the complex, we find here a very sober use of architectonic decoration. With the exception of the central hemicycle, the walls of the complex were almost exclusively decorated by the clean geometry of the doors, windows and balconies. The spaces provided for these elements lightened the mass, the joints and connecting points of which, due to the necessity of adapting to the irregularity of the ground, resulted in a kind of decoration with its daring interruptions and with the rhythmically flowing lines of the buildings.

Even if the Ulpian forum marked the final phase in the process of the growth and multiplication of open spaces in the monumental centre of Imperial Rome, it did not mark the end of projects which sought to restructure, restore or simply to integrate better the appearance of that most ancient public area in Rome, the republican forum. At the end of III century, a great monument appeared here, the Arch of Septimius Severus. This finished off the only corner of the square which was still without a monumental entrance, ant it was thus a companion to the other arches of Tiberius, Augustus, Gaius and Lucius. However, with this new arch the original function which the arch had had of passage or transit was lost. In addition to the practical and objective presence of steps, one should note here how the arch became in this case a simple support for honorary inscriptions which covered the entire attic, and for the figurative panels which celebrated the campaigns led by the emperor against the Parthians (194 and 198 A.D.).

The so-called *Umbilicus Urbis* is also from this period. This was a circular construction in brick located next to the Arch of Septimius Severus and was the indicator of the centre of the city, imitation of an analogous monument found in Greek cities.

The last phase of great forensic construction opened with the tetrarchy. The authority of the Senate was openly reaffirmed, out of reverence for tradition, by the restoration of the Curia under Diocletian. It was thus given that appearance of simple and austere space which can still be seen today, and which has even been accentuated by the loss of the portico along the facade and of the stucco covering which, by imitating ashlar-work, was supposed to have enlivened it.

And now, outside of what was strictly speaking the forum area, on a spot where, in the Flavian era, there had stood a complex of mercantile warehouses but which was nonetheless closely connected with the forum, here Maxentius built the last of the Roman basilicas. This was the only one which, breaking with tradition, used concrete for the internal covering. There was a central nave which ran in an east-west direction and which led to the western apse which was intended to contain the colossal statue of the emperor. This apse was characterized by three enormous cross vaults upon spans of the same height, buttressed by three rooms on each of the two sides, with barrel vaults (those on the north side are still visible). The work was completed and inaugurated by Constantine following his victory over Maxentius (312 A.D.). The original axis was however substituted by a transversal north-south one and the building was given a new entrance which was opened out of the middle room on the south side, along the Via Sacra, and an apse was added in line with this to the corresponding room on the north side. The small circular temple which was covered with a cupola and had an original façade punctuated by four niches, and which was located just to the west, should be seen in connection with the basilica. This was probably the Temple of the Penati, reconstructed by Constantine as a substitute for an earlier building consecrated to the cult of these ancient divinities which were linked to the Trojan legend. The earlier temple had been destroyed while the work was being carried out on the nearby basilica.

The last monument to be placed in the forum and which is conclusive in the history of this complex was the column erected in front of the *Rostra* in 608 A.D. by the Byzantine emperor, Foca. The column is however really from the II century A.D. and was thus re-utilized. Aside from the column, this emperor is worthy of remembrance only in virtue of the donation of the *Pantheon* to Pope Boniface IV who transformed it into a church and thus saved it from ruin. The figure of this emperor is otherwise linked to atrocious and bloody deeds.

Curtius hurls himself into the chasm;
relief by Lacus Curtius *in the Roman Forum
(Rome, Palazzo dei Conservatori).*

On the preceding pages and on these, a general view of the area of the Roman Forum. Seen here just as the excavations of the last one hundred years have presented it to us, it appears to be a complicated palimpsest of architectonic structures which is almost illegible by the layman because of the crowding and superimposition of these "signs" of a distant past. The hollow of the forum — the word comes from foras, meaning outside the inhabited area — at the foot of the Palatine hill, which was the earliest inhabited one, was, as far back as the Iron Age, a meeting and market place and also, in one part, a cemetery. This

area has then, from the time of its origins, united those two functions which have always characterized it: the sacred and the political-economic. The numerous monuments which testify to all the periods from the age of the kings to the late imperial one, are stratified in a complicated arrangement which modern excavations have investigated, reconstructing its appearance which was seriously altered by the havoc of the Middle Ages and of the Renaissance. The Roman Forum, called the Campo Vaccino, was in those times considered a quarry for building materials and the Popes and the great Roman families helped themselves to its contents. The authors of the "rediscovery" of the forum were the archaeologists Pietro Rosa, Giuseppe Fiorelli, Giacomo Boni, Alfonso Bartoli, Romanelli, Carrettoni and Fabbrini.

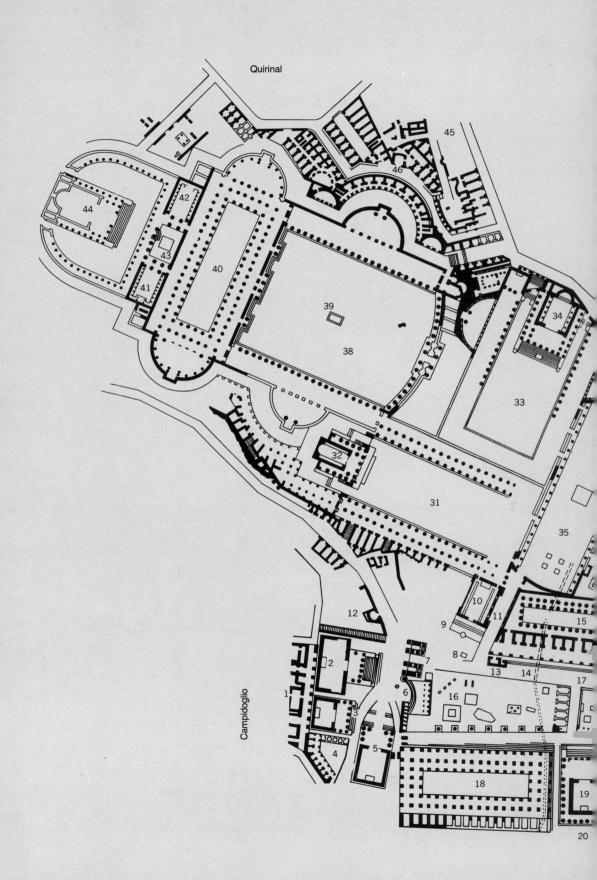

Quirinal

Campidoglio

20

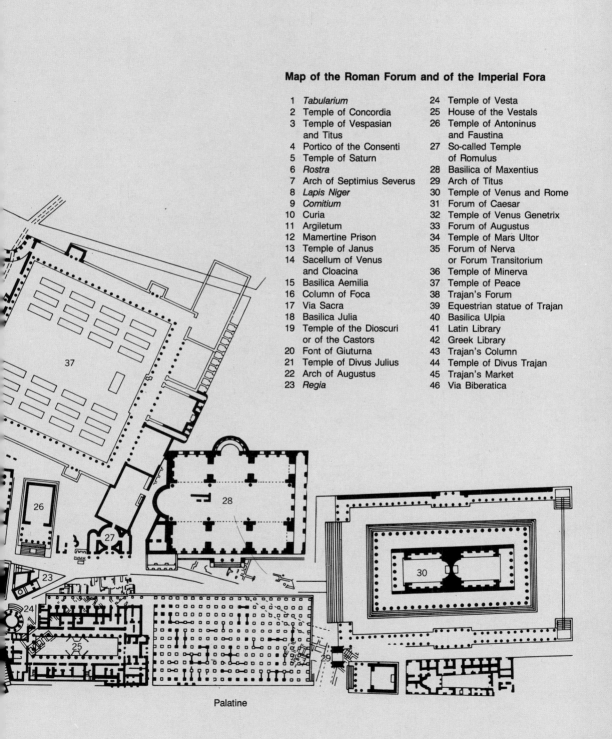

Map of the Roman Forum and of the Imperial Fora

1 *Tabularium*
2 Temple of Concordia
3 Temple of Vespasian
   and Titus
4 Portico of the Consenti
5 Temple of Saturn
6 *Rostra*
7 Arch of Septimius Severus
8 *Lapis Niger*
9 *Comitium*
10 Curia
11 Argiletum
12 Mamertine Prison
13 Temple of Janus
14 Sacellum of Venus
   and Cloacina
15 Basilica Aemilia
16 Column of Foca
17 Via Sacra
18 Basilica Julia
19 Temple of the Dioscuri
   or of the Castors
20 Font of Giuturna
21 Temple of Divus Julius
22 Arch of Augustus
23 *Regia*

24 Temple of Vesta
25 House of the Vestals
26 Temple of Antoninus
   and Faustina
27 So-called Temple
   of Romulus
28 Basilica of Maxentius
29 Arch of Titus
30 Temple of Venus and Rome
31 Forum of Caesar
32 Temple of Venus Genetrix
33 Forum of Augustus
34 Temple of Mars Ultor
35 Forum of Nerva
   or Forum Transitorium
36 Temple of Minerva
37 Temple of Peace
38 Trajan's Forum
39 Equestrian statue of Trajan
40 Basilica Ulpia
41 Latin Library
42 Greek Library
43 Trajan's Column
44 Temple of Divus Trajan
45 Trajan's Market
46 Via Biberatica

Palatine

In 1899, a roughly square zone paved in black marble was discovered in the area of the Comitium. Beneath this an archaic complex was brought to light (upper photo here on the right) with a sanctuary and tomb or heroon *containing a cippus which bears the oldest inscription in the Latin language written, in a bustrofedic manner, in Greek characters.*

The inscription on this Lapis Niger — *the black stone being the tomb of Romulus or an ancient shrine to an unknown divinity — has not yet been decisively integrated and deciphered, but it indicates that this place is sacred and fatal. The photo on the lower right shows the* Umbilicus Urbis, *the umbilicus or centre of the city, marked by a cylindrical building in brick work from the Severian era. The* Miliarium aureum *or the ideal point from which all distances were measured and from which all roads of the empire set out was a short distance from the Arch of Septimius Severus. It was marked by a column erected by Augustus, a fragment of which is shown on the opposite page in the lower photo. The upper photo on the same page shows the base of the* Equus Constantii *the equestrian monument of the emperor, near the Arch of Septimius Severus.*

On the following pages, the impressive and almost intact mass of the triumphal Arch of Septimius Severus built in 203 A.D. The arch consisted of three barrel vaults with an attic covered with a dedicatory inscription to Septimius Severus and Caracalla, who had returned victorious from the campaign against the Parthians the previous year. The architecture of the arch is in travertine and brick covered with sheets of marble and characterized by the presence of four "free" columns on high bases and by decorative and historical reliefs, the chiaroscuro effect of which is striking. The large panels above the small arches depict the most salient deeds of these two emperors and the taking of the Parthian cities of Seleucia, Edessa and Ctesifonte. The extrados of the large arches carry representations of Winged Victory and of the Genii of the Seasons, while those of the smaller arches carry representations of the rivers in keeping with Hellenistic models. The style of the reliefs already foreshadows the style of late antiquity, its lines being sketched summarily by sharp engravings and the reliefs being made up of large masses. The attic of the arch was crowned with a splendid bronze quadriga.

23

Here below, the base of the honorary column of the Tenth Anniversary of the Tetrarchy probably erected in 303 for the visit of the emperor Diocletian to Rome. The base is all that remains of this monumental complex and it carries on one of its four faces the inscription: "Caesarum decennalia feliciter". On the others there are scenes of libations to the god Mars and of sacrifices of priests and of the Senate made in the presence of the emperor. In the foreground of the photo on the opposite page, the colonnade of the Temple of Saturn and a view of the Basilica Julia.

All that remains of the ancient Basilica Julia, in the foreground of the photo here on the left, is the paved podium, the entrance steps and the lower joints of the columns. In the background of the same photo, the Temple of the Dioscuri. The Basilica was begun by Julius Caesar in 54 B.C. on the site of the earlier Basilica Sempronia, and it was later completed by Augustus. It was subsequently destroyed by fire on two occasions and rebuilt first by Augustus and then by Diocletian. The ruins of the colonnade of the Temple of the Dioscuri or of the Castors are from the reconstruction of the temple under Tiberius, but the cult, which was of Greek origin, existed in Rome and in Lazio as far back as the VI century B.C. as documents have proved. It is believed that here on this spot the two divine brothers appeared to announce the Roman victory of Lake Regillo in 496 B.C. and to water their horses at the font of Giuturna, near which the sanctuary dedicated to them was constructed.

Here on the right, the sacellum of the Font of Giuturna, identified in the Latin tradition with the nymph of the same name, sister of Turno.

The font assumed this monumental appearance in the republican era and was further adorned under Trajan and Severus.

Below, the meager ruins of the triumphal Arch of Augustus, the construction of which was decreed by the Senate following the battle of Anzio. The arch, which was erected in 29 B.C. had three openings: the central one was vaulted while the lateral openings had a flat covering. The tables of the Fasti consolari e trionfali *(shown here on the right) on which were inscribed the names of the consuls and victors from the beginning of the republic, were kept here. These were later moved to a room in the Palazzo dei Conservatori on the Campidoglio and incorporated into the architecture of Michelangelo.*

31

In 29 B.C., Octavian had a temple to Divus Julius, i.e. the divinized Julius Caesar constructed on the spot where the body of the emperor had been cremated. This was the first case in the history of Rome of divinization post mortem, a custom which came from the orient and which was to be used on a number of other occasions in the Empire. This temple to the Divus Julius (in the photo on these two pages) was probably corinthian with a cella preceded by six columns. In front of the pronaos there was a tribune for orators (Rostra ad divi Iulii) decorated with the pointed rostra from the Egyptian ships captured by Octavian at Anzio in 31 B.C. Inside the temple, in the cella, there was a statue of Caesar with a star upon its head, an image which was also represented on the front of the temple. All that remains of the temple are the ruins of the podium into which the circular altar used for the cremation was inserted and which is shown in the foreground of the photo. In the background the slopes of the Palatine hill can be seen, upon which, next to temples and other public buildings, stood the houses of illustrious citizens as well as the Domus Augustana, the residence of the emperors.

On the following page, a detail of the House of the Vestals with some sculptures of the chaste priestesses of the goddess. The House of the Vestals was an extensive complex which originally had a number of floors. It underwent a number of transformations and reconstructions, the most radical of which was carried out following the fire of Nero in 64 A.D. Connected to the House of the Vestals was the Temple of Vesta in which the sacred fire of the goddess, symbol of the very life of Rome, was kept. The temple, which is of very ancient origins and which according to tradition was founded along with the first walls of the city, was destroyed more than once. The appearance it has today corresponds to the last restoration which was carried out by Giulia Domna, wife of Septimius Severus following the fire of 191 A.D. It was a round building, surrounded by twenty corinthian columns and resting on a podium of opus caementium covered with marble. In an opening in the podium, the penus Vestae, a reliquary with the objects brought by Aeneas to Rome, was kept. The roof, which was conical, was open in the centre to allow the smoke to escape. The ruins of the temple are shown on page 35.

On the left, one of the statues in the atrium of the House of the Vestals. On the opposite page, a relief from the Basilica Aemilia, in the Antiquarium of the forum. The Basilica Aemilia, the only surviving republican basilica, which is shown on the following pages, was founded in 179 B.C. by M. Emilio Lepido and M. Fulvio Nobiliore. It was restored on a number of occasions by members of the gens Aemilia to the extent that it assumed the name by which we know it today. The Basilica, which was really a spacious covered area used to house the activities of the forum during inclement weather, derived its architectonic typology from Greek models, transmitted by the examples found in the colonies of southern Italy. It consisted of a large rectangular room divided into a series of naves by rows of columns which supported the roof. The central nave was higher than the others to allow for windows in the upper part. The Basilica Aemilia was preceded, on the side near the square, by a portico with a double row of columns off of which opened a row of shops. The photos at the bottom of pages 38 and 39 contain details of the pediment.

On these pages, the sober architecture of the Curia against the background of the Church of Saints Luca and Martina and looking onto the Comitium. The Curia, the meeting place of the Roman Senate, was founded, according to tradition, by king Tullus Hostilius and for this reason was called the Curia Hostilia. It was reconstructed in 80 B.C. by Sulla (Curia Cornelia), in 29 B.C. by Augustus (Curia Iulia) and finally by Diocletian following the fire of Carinus in 283 which destroyed a large part of the forum. In the VII century it was transformed into a Christian Church and dedicated to Saint Hadrian. The appearance which the building has today is the result of restoration carried out in the 1930's which eliminated the superstructures and restored the building to its original state, even though the stucco covering of the facade is missing. The bronze doors are copies of the original ones which in the XVII century were taken to St. John Lateran by Borromini. The interior consists of one large hall the ceiling of which is flat (the lacunar ceiling was reconstructed). The hall is 21 metres high, 18 metres wide and 27 metres long: these are more or less the proportions indicated in Vitruvius' work on architecture.

The height of this type of building, for acoustical reasons, was supposed to be equal to half of the sum of the lenght and the width. In the hall, one can still see three low wide steps along the walls; the seats of the approximately three hundred senators were set here.

The Curia houses today two large reliefs which were found in the centre of the forum and which are known as the plutei or anaglyphs of Trajan. These reliefs (see following pages) probably decorated the railing of a tribune and depict events from the reign of Trajan. The one shown in the upper photo depicts the Institution of the alimenta, i.e. agricultural loans at a very low interest rate which were awarded in exchange for foodstuffs for poor children. The lower photo shows the Destruction of the registers of back taxes as a result of the general pardon of the debts of the citizens. Both of these scenes are set in the forum and thus provide us with rare and precious testimony as to its original appearance. In both of these reliefs, one can note the statue of Marsia near the sacred fig tree which stood in the centre of the square. On the back of these reliefs, scenes of animals being led to sacrifice were sculpted.

The Temple of Concordia was constructed by Furius Camillus in 367 B.C. to celebrate the end of the struggle between the patricians and plebeians. It was later extensively restored by Tiberius (7-10 A.D.). Today nothing remains of this ancient edifice but the podium (shown below) and the threshold of the cella. Next to the Temple of Concordia was the Temple of Vespasian and Titus, dedicated to the two divinized emperors by the Senate and restored by Septimius Severus and Caracalla. Only three columns (shown on the opposite page) remain of this edifice which was made up of a spacious cella preceded by six columns.

Both of these sanctuaries stood at the foot of the Tabularium, *a grandiose building erected by the consul Q. Lutatius Catulus in 78 B.C. as a place to keep the archives of the ancient Roman state. It had been conceived at one time as a substructure for the citadel of the Capitoline and as a sort of scenic backdrop to the "stage" of the forum. This letter function is emphasized by the series of arches which opened up in the centre of the façade. In the XII century the Palazzo Senatorio, seat of the judgeship of the city, was constructed on the* Tabularium.

Here on the left, the great temple dedicated to Antoninus and Faustina, as the inscription on the front part of the architrave indicates. This building was erected in 141 A.D. by Antoninus Pius for the empress Faustina who died and was divinized in that same year. Later the emperor was included in this cult to his wife. This is the best conserved temple in the forum; the colonnade which rose on a high podium is still intact as is the cella within which the church of San Lorenzo in Miranda was built, in keeping with a common custom of the Middle Ages. Along the sides of the cell, completely constructed in peperino and later covered with sheets of marble, uncoils a sculpted frieze (details shown here on the right) in which figures of griffins facing candelabra alternate with coils of acanthus. The ten mighty monolithic columns of cipolin marble still present circular grooves around the upper part of their shafts where cords and ropes were twisted round them in an attempt to pull them down, most certainly in order to use them in some other construction. This was done in many parts of the forum, but with greater success, during the Middle Ages and the Renaissance.

In this photo, a detail of the front of the Temple of Antoninus and Faustina. In the foreground is the flight of stairs, reconstructed in brick, which led up to the high podium. In the centre of this flight of stairs is the ancient sacrificial altar in brick-work, and the mutilated statues in the spaces between the columns perhaps belonged to this temple. The typology of the Roman temple remained substantially unchanged from the Republican age through the late-Imperial age. This was the result of the fusion of autochthonous elements and elements of Greek-Hellenistic origin. But the classical elements — and this was always the case with Roman architecture — were incorporated into a new kind of synthesis. The frontal view of the building was given preference, and so the colonnade was limited to the frontal area of the temple which was raised on a high podium, this being part of the Italic heritage, with a flight of stairs at the front as well. The colonnade, the podium and the flight of stairs emphasize the one-directional axial concept of the structure, a concept opposite to that of the Greek temple which reached the apex of its typology in the peripteral form, with the various sides being integrated, organic and undifferentiated.

Below, the Basilica of Maxentius, begun by this emperor on the hill of the Velia near the Via Sacra and on the site of the Horrea Piperataria, *the spice warehouses. This was completed in 324 A.D. by Constantine who however altered the planimetry by changing the original axis. The building, the ruins of which are limited to its north side, was one of the most grandiose of Imperial Rome. It had a rectangular form (100×65 metres) and was subdivided into three naves, each with three spans, square in the central nave and rectangular in the lateral ones.*

In the northern part of the Basilica of Maxentius, shown here in the photo on the left, the barrel vaults of its three vast rooms are still intact. The external wall of the central room curves into an apse with niches which once contained statues. Another apse was located on the western side and in it, the colossal acrolitic statue of Constantine was placed. Just the head of this statue, the remains of which are in the Palazzo dei Senatori, was over two metres high. Below, a view of the eastern front of the basilica.

The photo on the following pages shows the attic of the Arch of Titus, erected during the reign of Domitian to celebrate the triumph in Judea. Inside the one arch of this monument there are two large reliefs which deal with the theme of this triumph by showing two moments of the procession: one with the emperor with the Goddess Rome and the Genius of the Senate and of the people of Rome, riding on his chariot, and the other with marching soldiers carrying the treasures taken from Jerusalem.

The reliefs on the inside of the vault of the Arch of Titus represent an important chapter and qualitative turning point as far as Roman art is concerned (details on these two pages). The soft and atmospheric modelling, the organization of the figures in an arrangement which was no longer on a plane parallel to that of the observer but rather on spherical portions of the surface or along diagonal perspectives in order to create a real sense of space — almost a XV century stiacciato: all this marked the abandonment of the cold classicism of the Augustan age in favour of a new and naturalistic vision rendered with expert technique. The various figures stand out against the background which is transformed by a few indications from a solid and compact band into an atmospheric and engaging cavity with the varying depths of the relief being executed with naturalness and skill.

The ruins of the Temple of Venus and Rome, at the eastern end of the forum, are a grandiose testimony to the intense building activity which was going on under the emperor Hadrian. This temple was begun in the year 121, but it still had not been completed when this emperor died in 138. Hadrian himself had worked with Apollodorus of Damascus in the planning of the temple, and it was due to disagreement over this planning that the two men broke off their relationship and Apollodorus fell into disgrace. The mass of this temple, which is the most imposing one of ancient Rome, was the result of the union of two twin temples which were back to back, that is with the apses of the relative celle up against one another. The covering of this double temple (the total lenght of which measured 164.90 metres) with a lacunar barrel vault necessitated the construction of perimetral walls of great thickness, which were lightened on the inside by niches with statues, and marked off by a colonnade. They were completely covered with coloured marble. On these pages, a view of one of the two celle the apse of which still presents traces of the rich lacunar decoration.

Here on the right, a
fragment of the frieze from
the Temple of Venus
Genetrix which is kept in
the Palazzo dei
Conservatori. This fragment
with putti dates from the re-
building of the temple under
Trajan, and it testifies to the
quality of relief work, with
great vivacity and colour.
The construction of the
Temple of Venus Genetrix,
at the end of one of the
lesser sides of the Forum of
Caesar which had already
been begun, was decided
after the battle of Farsalo in
48 B.C. and marked a
precise ideological turning
point in the idea of the
"prince" who, with the
propagandistic exaltation of
the offspring of the gens
Iulia, discendent of Venus,
assumed for himself a sacred
function and a divine
nature. As far as urbanistic
typology was concerned, the
temple as the ideal spatial
completion of the forum and
as the fulcrum of a perfect
scenic organization, was to
become from this moment
on a fundamental and
central element also from an
ideological point of view
expressing, in imitation of
the many sanctuaries of the
Hellenistic Orient, the
divine presence of the
emperor.

The Forum of Caesar was originally built near a hill which linked the Campidoglio with the Quirinal hill, but which was later levelled by Trajan. This forum had a rectangular shape (measuring 160×75 metres) with a double colonnaded portico along three sides (the photo on this page shows the south-west side). The fourth side of the forum was occupied by the Temple of Venus Genetrix which was built up against the hill at the end of the square. Three corinthian columns (shown here on the left) are all that remain of the temple. This forum was dedicated to Venus in 46 B.C. It was however completed by Augustus and largely reorganized by Trajan.

The Forum of Augustus took up once again the planimetry of Caesar's forum, with a rectangular square closed off at the end by a temple. Augustus dedicated the temple to Mars Ultor, i.e. Mars the avenger of the death of Caesar. It was an eight-columned temple with corinthian columns along three sides, resting on a high podium (shown below and in the detail in the upper photo on the next page). In order to clearly separate the forum from the populated areas behind it and also to create a sort of barrier against fires, Augustus enclosed the entire complex with a mighty wall which created a kind of scenographic backdrop (the lower photo on the next page shows a detail of this).

On these pages, photos of a rhinoceros, a goat and a bull: three of the seven colossal animal heads kept in the Roman National Museum and which probably come from Trajan's forum. This forum, the largest of all the Roman forums (300 metres long and 185 metres wide), was built by the emperor between 107 and 113 A.D. cutting away the hill which united the Campidoglio with the Quirinal hill. The architect of this grandiose complex was Apollodorus of Damascus who changed from the layout of the preceding fora by placing at the end of this one not a temple but a basilica, thus copying the central squares of Roman military encampments. There were also two libraries, one Latin and the other Greek, which were also derived from a military model. These libraries framed the Basilica Ulpia which was situated on the spot where in the castrum *the military archives would have been found. Finally, the column, located between the two libraries, occupied the spot where the colours of the legion would have been displayed in an encampment. In addition to the column, there was also a temple dedicated to Divus Trajan, built however only after his death.

Along the main sides of the Forum of Trajan opened two exedrae, once paved in marble (below, a detail of the paving). The north-eastern one was concentric with the complex of Trajan's Market, a complex of buildings on various levels which was the commercial centre of the city as well as serving as the substructure of the Quirinal (photo on following pages). At the lowest level there is a large exedra, completely built of brick, with openings of eleven tabernae along the lower part. This exedra terminated at

each of the two ends in an apsed room two storeys high. A third floor which was set back in relation to the first two looked onto the street behind it, the Via Biberatica. From this street, by means of a steep stairway, access was provided to the second part of the complex, made up of a large hall with a six-crossed vaulted ceiling (a detail is shown on the opposite page). Here there was a series of rooms on two floors which were probably used as offices for the direction of this entire complex and, in part, as a warehouse.

On this page, a view of the Via Biberatica, one of the best conserved areas of ancient Rome. This street, which takes its name from the late-Latin noun biber (drink), was probably full of shops and places of business that provided refreshments. Some of these still have the travertine cornices around the doorways. On the opposite page, a photo of Trajan's column, the only monument from the forums which has come down to us practically intact. Only the statue on the top was replaced during the Middle Ages by the present one of St. Peter. The column, which was constructed of large blocks of marble, measures 40 metres and rests on a high pedestal decorated with trophies. Inside there is a small room which can be entered and where the urn containing the ashes of Trajan was deposited.

A relief uncoils along the shaft of the column of Trajan. It depicts the Dacian Wars (101-102 and 105-107) which are here described not only to celebrate the victory, but also in a documentary fashion, so much so that it is believed that they were based on the Commentarii of Trajan himself. This hypothesis has found support both from the fact that the Commentarii were contained in one of the two libraries of the forum and also from the very form of the relief which reproduces that of an antique book, a scroll (volumen) wrapped in a spiral fashion around a column. For Roman sculpture, this was an entirely new form. The reliefs, which were originally polychromatic, raccount all of the phases of the wars in minute detail, from the Crossing of the river Danube (on the opposite page) to the construction of the encampments, the battles and the overcoming of the enemy chiefs. Here on the left, The Roman cavalry chases Decebalus (the reliefs here reproduced are plaster copies of the originals, found in the Roman national Museum). The story of the two wars is separated by the figure of Victory in the act of writing on a shield. The column is the work of the so-called Master of the works of Trajan, and dates from the year 113.

Index